People willing to obtain the Master

Title and to open theyr own school

please contact me on:

d1mart@yahoo.es

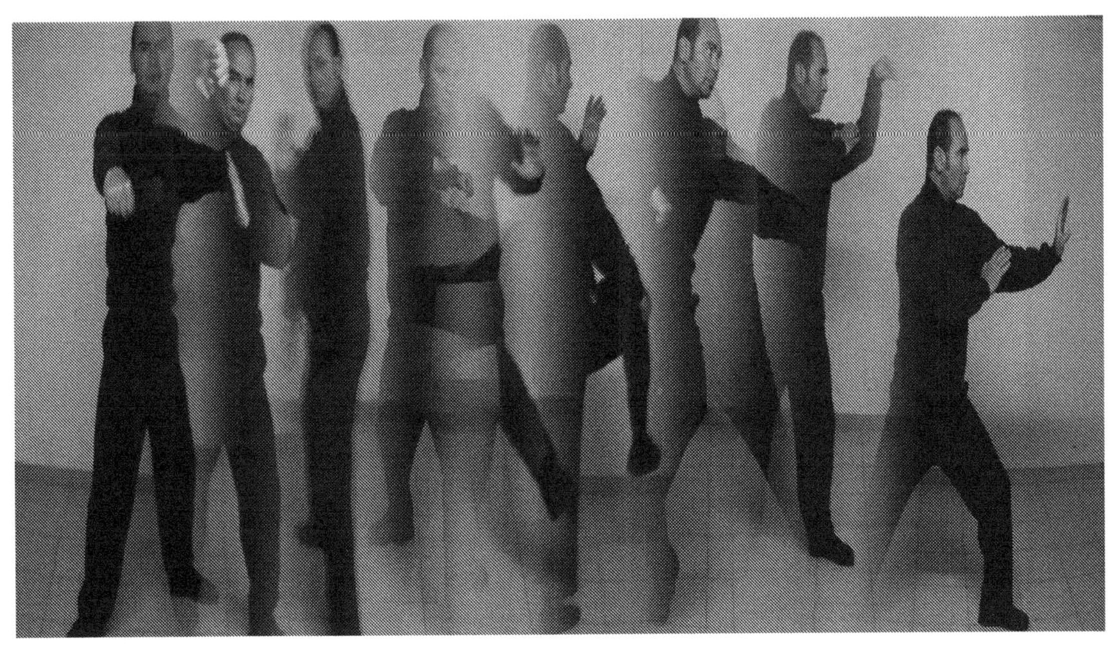

Order this book online at www.trafford.com/07-2422
or email orders@trafford.com

Most Trafford titles are also available at major online book retailers.

Note for Librarians: A cataloguing record for this book is available from Library and Archives Canada at www.collectionscanada.ca/amicus/index-e.html

ISBN: 978-1-4251-5433-2

We at Trafford believe that it is the responsibility of us all, as both individuals and corporations, to make choices that are environmentally and socially sound. You, in turn, are supporting this responsible conduct each time you purchase a Trafford book, or make use of our publishing services. To find out how you are helping, please visit www.trafford.com/responsiblepublishing.html

Our mission is to efficiently provide the world's finest, most comprehensive book publishing service, enabling every author to experience success. To find out how to publish your book, your way, and have it available worldwide, visit us online at www.trafford.com/10510

www.trafford.com

North America & international
toll-free: 1 888 232 4444 (USA & Canada)
phone: 250 383 6864 ♦ fax: 250 383 6804 ♦ email: info@trafford.com

The United Kingdom & Europe
phone: +44 (0)1865 722 113 ♦ local rate: 0845 230 9601
facsimile: +44 (0)1865 722 868 ♦ email: info.uk@trafford.com

10 9 8 7 6 5 4 3 2 1

TAUDANC

Self defence and Health

SPANISH MARTIAL ARTS

Cover photograph: Dan Giuglea, Relief painting
" THE MODERN MAN"

Dedicated to

Gheorghiu Adriana and Gheorghiu Anton,

who has given me so much support,

to my sons Stelian and Salvador Jesús,

to God who is in everything,

to Spain and its culture for inspiring me,

to the wonderful people of Alicante.

Thanks to my two Bull - terrier dogs Picky and

Rock for all the unconditional love that they give to us.

WARNING

The author and the editors of this work will under no circumstance accept responsibility for injuries or other damages that may occur due to the reading or during the practise of the contents of this book.

Physical activities or activities of another type,
described and shown in this book may be difficult or dangerous for some people, for which the reader is advised to consult with his or her doctor before beginning the practise.

It is advisable to consult your doctor especially for those people who suffer from asthma, heart disease, anxiety or
other illnesses where physical exercise is not recommended.

CONTENTS

AUTHOR'S NOTE

Life in modern society makes us forget to look after our health, or leaves us little time to do so. In the past few years Chinese relaxation techniques have been used in the workplace, but the truth is that it is not necessary to follow a set practise plan , "X", but to practise some movements slowly or using 50% strength, combined with good breathing and concentration.

TAUDANC has emerged to contribute its grain of help in this sense by being a source of health.
This book is aimed especially at normal everyday people who do not have a sports background or time to practise a sport nor time to learn how to get on in a gym. TAUDANC combines defence techniques with meditation, with its specific movement's interpreted Tai-Chi style.

All this combined with the simplicity of practising it anywhere, at anytime, without the necessity of specific sportswear.
What you do need is to make the most of your free time and your willingness to learn to learn.
You have to stop and think about doing something different from what you usually do, each day, each week, and each year.

You must put your life in order, be positive and recognise that you have to adapt the control of your life to the different situations that are presented to you over time.

TAUDANC is not restricted by any rule or order of performance or practise.
It does not impose timetables neither does it follow the rigid norms of martial arts practise.

You are free to practise it how and when you wish. There are no rules.
Neither is there rules and plans to defend you.
No martial art ritual is necessary.
It is not necessary to give spectacular kicks, on the contrary with little effort, a few movements and with some efficient techniques you will be safe.
Spectacular is not the term for this style, efficient is. You should aim for the practical, not the sensational nor the spectacular.

With this first book of introduction to TAUDANC I hope to provide what some people have been seeking for a long time.

Maybe it will be the "something" of many , that covers the emptiness in their souls, or simply make them even healthier.

1. Introduction

During the passage of time, man, for necessity or for ingenuity, man created ways to defend himself which in time was called Martial Arts. Over time they began to be practised to enjoy good health or simply to maintain the spirit alive.

Thus, in Japan, the peasants looked for a way to defend themselves from thieves and invaders. They had no weapons nor time to make them and had to defend themselves with what they had, agricultural tools such as:- the nunchaku, used to thresh rice, short sticks, long sticks, the tonfa, wooden swords etc.

Something similar happened in China; inspired by animal fighting Kung-Fu was created. All these techniques have been developed, modified and improved over time. Nowadays there exist around two thousand styles and branches of Kung-Fu. TAUDANC is inspired by martial arts, but has been adapted to the necessities of our times. In the past seven years I have studied the style of fighting of the man against the bull, of the bull against the man and that of the Bull Terrier dog.

Each one has its own technique: the man's being to wear down his opponent bit by bit and to win or to give a winning blow, the bull's to defend itself by attacking, the butting, the Bull Terrier's, that by its particular character-stubborn-is prepared to fight anywhere, in any circumstance, with total control, does not even let go when it bites.

TAUDANC style has been created developing and combining these three techniques, but due to the lack of lightness another technique inspired by the Flamenco dance has been added.

With this latest addition a technique has been created with movements full of gentleness, harshness, avoidance and of expectation for the blow of mercy, at times counter-attacking like the bull fighter that dodges with total certainty, anticipating the movements of the bull. By using and adapting these defence techniques a different style has been created, comfortable and efficient, healthy, and at the same time being easy to practise. If the Chinese have been inspired by animal fighting to create Kung-Fu why not create a style inspired in what we have: bulls, bull fighters and Flamenco? We all remember that Karate and Kung –Fu gave much to talk about in the 1970's , with films that brought us new knowledge, ways of movement, of thinking, opening up to us a new horizon towards the practises that contribute to and maintain health.

2. Description

TAUDANC is composed of a careful selection of the best techniques from the wide range of martial arts studied in the past 24 years, some of them having been practised during all of this time.
In addition to this the previously mentioned techniques have been added:-
- That of the bull and the bull fighter.
- That of the bull terrier,
- That of the Flamenco dance.

It has been created and adapted to our modern day life, offering us three parts which are at once defining and unifying:-
- Sport as self defence,
- Meditation,
- Concentration.

The style of the techniques and the Tai _Chi style relaxation brings us health, self control and self esteem, strengthening the body when practising them.
Meditation and relaxation keep our spirit alive and active, it makes it productive, while the self defence strengthens and maintains health.
You will feel like an actor and a spectator at the same time.
It contains gentle techniques, techniques that are practised with 15% strength, but there are also others which are harder where 100% strength is used.

It can practically be adapted to any type of person, each one can practise the part which most adapts to his or her character, or the whole set can be practised if that is preferred.
It shows you how to protect yourself at all times from attacks from your opponent, making the most of the weak points of each blow, of not wasting energy unnecessarily.

TAUDANC combines gentleness with strength and speed; each technique may be carried out in various ways with the adequate breathing.
The gentle speed of the movements of the bull fighter or of a Flamenco dancer, combined with the harshness and strength of the bull, the speed and the ferocious attack of the Bull Terrier. The blocking techniques like those of dodging are characterized by gentleness, administering only the necessary force to lead the adversary towards where your attack/blow is directed, leaving the field free. Movements are quick and generally unexpected by the opponent. The rolling and dodging techniques combined with the counter attack are the ones that best describe the style.

3. Concept and Philosophy

**The basic concept is to save movement, spend energy only when necessary, and use your opponent's energy. Practise movements that you have never practised before, that you didn't even know existed.
All martial arts are related to chess.**

**The basis of chess is warfare, martial arts is related to that. A very simple equation, in short, both have common principals.
Let's number some:-**

1. Do not expose yourself when attacking.

2. Make sure that each blow has a target.

3. Do not ignore or undervalue your adversary, nor his movements.

4. Avoid your enemy's strong points.

5. Look for the weak points.

6. Try to fool your opponent.

7. Do not attack with only one blow in mind.

8. Break through your opponent's defence.

9. Cover your plans.

10. Try to win step by step.

11. If you are weak appear strong.

12. If you are strong appear weak.
We never know when we will need to defend ourselves, neither where nor how it will happen, or when it will end, for this reason we must train our

mind so that we are always prepared.

Once TAUDANC is in your mind, your actions will make your arms, legs and elbows move. As if you had been born with the gift of defending yourself, you will do it as if it were: - natural, instinctive, involuntary, and reflexive, just like the feeling of hunger, of moving a hand to scratch yourself, moving a foot to be able to walk. It is now part of you.
Your arms will act on their own as if they had a mind of their own, they will know how to act adequately in each situation.

There does not exist or there should not exist a premeditated plan of attack or defence, you should not prepare yourself for what is going to happen, let your mind relax, your arms will know what to do.

Let your opponent attack and let your hands and feet act by themselves.
Instinct and practise will guide you.
Do not try to prepare in your mind a certain combination “x”, the solution is to prepare nothing, you will act according to the situation.

4. Movements and Steps

Bearing in mind the defence of the "safe zone" (where it is supposed that the opponent cannot reach you, considered to be 1.5m of distance between him and yourself), movements are classified by:-

1. **defence**
2. **attack**
3. **counter-attack**
4. **Interception of blow.**

These movements will be applied with each one of the techniques that we are going to introduce in the following pages.
The techniques may be carried out with or without these movements according to each individual situation.
Body weight is different for each movement or position. As a general rule, the weight distributed in the defence positions is that of 60/40% and that of 75/25% putting more weight on the back leg and respectively less weight on the front leg. When in attack the weight distribution is the opposite to when in defence, more weight on the front leg and less on the back, as a general rule the percentages are as indicated above.
In a counter-attack the weight distribution changes in respect to the defence or attack distribution. We have here a variation of weight distribution from 10 to 100% depending on each technique used.
In blow interception the body weight distribution on the legs will be divided 50/50% and 70/30 %. 70% on the front foot depending on the situation and technique used.

STEPS

In general the steps are related to the applied technique, therefore we have:-
- **Steps forward, steps back.**
- **Right side, left side.**
- **Rotation steps.**
- **Turns.**

All these steps are performed at an angle between 5 and 180 degrees of movement and rotation in relation with the centre of the body weight, defined by the two co-ordinates "x" and "y" in combination with the possible movements: front, back, sides, depending on the techniques which are used.

POSITIONS AND STEPS

General:-Basic and combat, these being the two basic groups. Here onwards they are classified depending on the added technique.
The positions have their weight spread out and the steps have their angles between 45-90 degrees.
The steps may be taken in different directions but the main thing is that you always adopt an advantageous position from where you can defend or attack.

BASIC POSITION

This is where it all begins; it is the basic element, the entrance door to a new world. The basic position spreads the body weight by 50%, legs lightly bent, back leaning forward, the spine straight, relaxed.

Be light as a feather to be able to move with speed hands, legs, head and other elements that can help you defend yourself.

COMBAT POSITION

Feet at 1.5 the width of the shoulders, a light position but under control.
Left hand defending the face and the abdomen, right hand forward the same as the leg. Ready to stop and to attack.
Weight distribution 55-45% on the back leg, back slightly bent, chin close to chest.
The legs must never be in line, always at a distance of 15-25cm.

5. Basic Techniques

A. HAND TECHNIQUES
B. KICKS
C. COUNTER-ATTACK
D. DIRECT TECHNIQUES
E. BLOCKING TECHNIQUES
F. PATCHES
G. LEG CUTS
H. PRESSURE TECHNIQUES
I. THRUSTS
J. THROWINGS
K. ROLLINGS
L. DODGES
M. ATTACK
N. BULTER TECHNIQUES
O. OPRESSIVE TECHNIQUES

A. HAND TECHNIQUES

STRAIGHT BLOW

From the basic position, we raise the right arm with a fist formed to chest height.
The left hand in prepared rearguard, from here it moves forwards with a turn of 180º.
The overall movement should be both arms going back and forwards at the same time, both having the corresponding rotation.
The blow can be performed with or without the light twisting of the hip in the opposite direction of the fist which is hitting.

HAMMER BLOW

From the same base position, the head is turned to the right to locate the opponent.
The right arm is bent forwards close to the body with the fist at chin level towards the face.
From here you deploy towards the right with a turn of 90º in such a way that the form of the hand called "Hammer" strikes in a position parallel to the ground.
Maximum hand extension is not recommended.

SIDE BLOW WITH THE KNUCKLES

Movement goes from down to up with a fist turn of 90º.

The body moves forwards as much as necessary.

The strength of the blow is generated by the speed of how it is delivered.
The hand makes a to and fro movement, the arm stretches out and contracts.

INVERTED FIST

The movement starts from below, as it begins to rise the fist turns inwards.

The left hand is situated in an excellent position, being ready to stop or to strike.

The knuckles are used to strike. Both movements are performed at the same time, the blow and the simulation of blocking with the left hand.

Strength used 30/50%. All the power of the blow must be produced by speed.

KNIFE HAND BLOW

This type of blow is intended for the throat, but is efficient in any part of the body.

It is also used as a block, one blow against another blow, being applied as a side blow.

From the base position, if you bend your arm and then extend it you have performed the technique.

It is advisable to apply a "knife" turn.
Used in attack the strength is of 70%, in defence the strength of the arm is much less.

ELBOW BLOW

Elbow blows are sharp, hard blows of much impact.

They are easy to carry out and are used at a short distance, as a defence against blows, kicks and as attack.

They are applied in various directions from inside out, from outside in.

In the photograph the left hand hides a block followed by an elbow blow.
The weight balance is 60/40% on the front leg, back leg slightly bent.

SIMPLE OR DOUBLE PALM BLOW

It is used as an attack, as a continuation from a previously used block.
The palms of the hands are used to strike and can be applied in two ways:- as short blows full of strength on a short impact or with 80% of strength as a short push. Arms slightly bent, back leg steady.
Weight distribution 65/35% on the back leg. The blow is usually applied in the chest area, however, it can be applied to the stomach or the back.

B. KICKS

FRONTAL KICK

It is composed of two actions performed as if one.

The first one consists in raising the bent leg, the supporting leg slightly bent.

The second action consists in moving the leg forwards.

This is the starting point for performing the front kick. The back leg will apply the frontal kick.
At the moment of application the sole of the right foot will move forwards resting on the toes and part of the sole. The front kick may be applied two ways:-
1.In two actions performed as if one, the aim being to push strongly.
2. In two actions much defined one from the other; in this case movement must be of high speed impact.
In both cases at the moment of the second action the body leans back at the same time that the foot extends and touches its target.
Regarding the second option of performance, the knuckles of the fingers face back when hitting, obtaining a stronger impact and shortening distance.

SIDE KICK

Composed of two actions-

1. Starting from the combat position the forward leg is withdrawn bending it at the knee at abdomen level.

2. In continuation stretch out at the same time as rocking the body towards the back forming the counter weight, also the balance of the body necessary not only for performance but to maintain poise at the moment of impact.

Two types of balance can be spoken about thought up to help and maintain the body still at the moment of impact Balance for performance and balance of the performance at the moment of impact.
In the opposite case the body would go backwards and the kick would lose effect. If you do not get the impact right because of miscalculating the distance of the opponent there will be an unbalance causing an exaggerated movement forwards.

CIRCULAR KICK

The previous photograph with the raised knee is the starting point.

The difference between the side and the circular kick is the circular movement applied to this technique, from outside towards the inside.

It may be applied at various levels such as head, abdomen or feet, as shown in the photograph.

It is also composed of two actions reducing the difference between them as much as possible.

BACKWARDS KICK

With the knee raised and the opponent situated behind, the leg is extended back at the same time as balancing the body towards the front and the head turning
towards the opponent.

It is a very useful technique to cover the body.
There are two ways to perform:-

1. Kicking in a straight line.

2. Applying the blow from below upwards with the leg steady and without the withdrawal and deploy factor.

IN & OUT KICKS

The IN & Out's: In the IN kick the leg at the back is used while in the OUT kick the leg in front is used. In both, a semi circular path is traced facing out or facing in. At the time of performance the supporting foot must be slightly bent with the sole resting on the toes. The hands carry out a movement of 15-20º in the opposite direction to the kick. Balance is maintained applying the necessary rocking.

ROTATORY KICK

The left foot makes a circular movement turning backwards First the hip begins the movement followed by the foot. The technique consists in a rotation and an approaching of the right foot towards the opponent.
There are two ways of performing:-
1. Applying the blow with the foot forming a hook adding to it the rapid withdrawal action of the knee.
2. The same turning movement with the foot steady like a metal bar wiping out everything in its path.
In the second action the foot returns to the initial position.
In the first type of action, after hook kicking, the leg lands a step away towards the front.

HOOK KICK

From the base position turn towards the left until having a side position with the opponent.

From here hit upwards with the leg performing a hook.

The head will be facing towards the adversary as far as possible.

C. COUNTER-ATTACK

The name of this technique may be interpreted in the following way:-
- counter, an action against your attacker, be it a block or the application of a technique.
- Attack, the answer to the action from the opponent using blows or combined techniques. You may counter-attack with or without movements, with or without blocks. Depending on the attack of the opponent, a simple classification may be done:-
1. Counter-attacks of short reach, 2. of medium reach, 3. of long reach, 4. a combination of the above with double blow or a combination of block and blow at two different levels. Counter-attacks are many and multiple, of various compositions, or simple blows applied at various levels.
You can counter-attack against reception of a short reach attack with a block and a knee blow. It is recommended to use long reach counter-attacks against short reach blows. For example: Against an attack with the hand, counter-attack with a side kick. Depending on the situation of combat counter-attacks may also be dislocations, pushes or other techniques not denominated as blows.
There are no rules; the fight in itself creates a unique situation because each fight is unique, like a work of art, done by the same author but with a pause in between performances.

Examples of counter-attack.

1. Blocking of hand blow and application of side kick.
Two action technique involving all the factors that contribute to the performance: - displacement, balance, breathing for the block and for the kick, focus on the destination of the adversary's blow and of your own.
It is advisable to pay attention to the place where your foot is going to land, once the kick has been executed.
Eyes must not follow the blocking or kicking movements, always having a very open visual field and keeping them fixed a meter behind the opponent.
Try to act by instinct, not following or reacting to the adversary's movements which may be mistaken.

2. Outward hand blocking and application of straight or circular knee kick.

From the base position the foot in front is withdraw decreasing the distance between the feet at the same time and blocking with the forearm or the palm of the hand towards the outside or inside.

The front foot resting on the toes and part of the sole.

The right hand is nearer to the chin and the chin is resting on the shoulder, the back leaning forwards.

3. Outward or inward blocking and application of chest straight blow.

Blocking to the outside or to the inside with short movements from below upwards. Blocks and blows can be carried out separately or may be carried out at the same time.

Being a counter-attack it is understood that the opponent has moved towards us. Weight distribution: - 60% on the front leg, 40% on the back leg.

The movement of the shoulder and fist is to try to direct the blow to the side where the attacker's arm is.

4. Inside block and blow to the genitals with the palm of your hand.

The body moves forwards.
The two techniques are performed 100% face forward.

The right hand is held vertically from top to bottom and has a circular movement while the body weight is distributed by 70% on the front leg and 30% on the back.

The set of movements is propelled by the hip and the change of position of the soles of the feet.

5. Counter-attack by applying dodging and butting the end result being that the man hits the opponent's chest.

Butting may be applied by flexing one of the front feet.

Pay attention to the block which I am doing with my knee.

Another very important point is the position of the left hand which may continue with a blow after the butting if this has not obtained the desired effect.

6. Side kick block with left hand and "knife" blow to the throat.

Passing from the combat position to the defence position with weight distribution between 50/50% and 60/40% on the back foot.
Hip movement at a 15-30º angle towards the left.
If the rotation angle of the hip is increased, performance will only be possible moving the right foot towards the right or the left foot to the back following the direction of the opponent's kick.
Try not to exceed the angle indicated without the adequate foot movement.

D. DIRECT TECHNIQUES

We have seen in previous pages that there are many techniques where two actions are performed together. For example: a block and a blow simultaneously. This is the principle of the direct technique, applying two techniques as if one at the same time, but always after your opponent has initiated the attack. Direct techniques are those that I personally like most and are frequent techniques of TAUDANC.
They are made up of two parts:-
1.Soft-hard, this combines for example, soft blocks with hard blows and kicks, both applied at the same time of course.
2. Hard, this part uses blocking techniques using 100% strength. They are not flexible and are designed to break the attack. Many fights end the instant this technique is used on arms and legs, leaving the opponent unable to use them for some time. Next we are going to see some examples of these techniques.

Soft-hard technique

The block has been done gently using it only to divert the opponent's blow. The strength of the straight blow that is performed has only half the strength, the opponent contributes the other half by moving forwards while trying to reach his target, in this case our chest. The technique has been applied without movement. If the blow received is stronger, movement in one of the four cardinal points is applied.

In this picture we are seeing application of the direct blow technique with movement to the back or to the front.
So that the technique may be performed correctly attention must be paid to the calculation of the impact of the opponent's chest against our fist.
Some practise is needed until the force of both elements hit each other, at the right time, full of energy.

We have here a hand block against a blow and the right foot carrying out a blow or a leg cut against the front leg of the opponent.
Another example of direct technique using another application, the foot.
The hand that blocks goes to the outside while the blow applied
with the leg on the leg of the attacker is directed inwards or to the front.
If it is a blow with the foot, there are two ways of applying:- with strength, pushing inwards or to the front or simply as a stopping blow.

A block or a blow directed to the chest and in reply a blow applied to the throat with the heel of the hand.

Block and blow, both inwards. It can be done with rotary movement of the right foot towards the right or left foot to the front or to the back.

Hard Technique

It can easily be seen in the photograph the hardness in both the block and blow action. As we have mentioned, there is a time which separates the two parts of the performance using all the existing force separately.

Back leg slightly bent, weight distribution 60/40% on the front foot. Just by looking at the mouth you can judge the amount of air which has been expelled so as to be able to administer strength to the block and the blow and also to be able to strengthen the movement and stability of the position.
A clear example of a very hard block
directed at a stomach kick or a blow with the same target.

The block is strong and begins its movement some 30cms back, next to the right ear, following a downward path with corresponding rotation. The left hand is prepared for a blow that may be straight towards the throat or may be aimed at the same attacking factor.

E. BLOCKING TECHNIQUES

The fundaments of the blocking techniques are the direction of the applications.

Guided by this rule we will have:-
-outside blocks,
- Inside blocks, to these can be added:-
-downwards,
- upwards (the least used) being substituted many times by dodging techniques.
Blocking instruments are: hands, legs, arms, elbows, knees and the soles of the feet.
Next we will show some selected blocks: - hand and foot which may be used as a defence and are very easy to apply.

In the photograph, a simple technique of a hand block going from down upwards, from inside to out.

The block is done with the edge of the hand or with the forearm. It may be applied with or without movement.

In the photograph is the same block, but carried out from the top downwards.
The part which is blocking is the whole of the forearm, length wise or only the side of the palm.
Block from the top downwards with the palm.
The only object of blocking is to divert the kick or the blow downwards, allowing it to follow the initial path without strength.
With this we hope to achieve the diversion of the attack and at the same time the unbalancing of the opponent.

This is the applied diversion; look at the position in which the opponent's arm has arrived.
In blocking from outside in, a rotation of 90º of the forearm has been applied to facilitate the diversion and have minimum contact.

Inside forearm block.
From the combat position a left turn is made, at the same time as the deflecting block.

Leg block against inside kicks.
The leg that usually performs the block is the front one; however it can be done from the back.
The idea is to follow your opponent's straight kick with your leg lightly bent.
Careful with the body rocking!

Another block with the foot in the starting phase of trying to kick.
Movement from the outside to the inside at the same time with a gentle rise.
It is a way of hooking the leg of your opponent. A soft upward pull is applied.
Again we are talking about diverting the direction. The difference between the previous technique and this one is that the foot makes a hook situating itself under the attacker's foot.

Foot block against an attempt to overtake, initiated by the opponent.
You simply raise the knee to a distance of 30cm and open it towards the opponent's knee.
It is not a blow, but a "stopping blow" type of movement, having as a target the attacker's femur.

Other stopping block applied to the knee of the opponent who is in the starting phase of his kick.

Elbow block-.

Very efficient on many occasions leaving free range for a multitude of counter-attack combinations.
It is also used as a blow in short distances.
It is carried out with the rotation of the hip in the desired direction at the same time that the positions of the soles of the feet are changed. The body weight is distributed 50/50%, the right leg semi flexed, left hand prepared to block or strike.

Goose neck block

Highly valued technique for its easy transformation to a blow towards the throat in record time given the proximity of the opponent. You can hit, using the tips of your fingers, only the thumb, the fist or the knuckles of the bent fingers. Left hand supporting with its strength the arm that blocks it, situated at the same time in an ideal position to defend or strike. The strength of support of the left hand increases or diminishes depending on the opponent's attack. Example:-
To block a direct blow use less force, to block a kick, use maximum force of support with the increase of the distance between the legs. The movement goes from down upwards and outwards. The block is done with the forearm.
A forward movement is recommended at the moment of the blow.

Block to the head against kick,

The hand prepared to strike after blocking.
Left hand extended to control the closing in of the opponent.
At the moment of performance we pass from combat position to defence position, that is, the body weight distributed will reach 60/40% on the back foot. This also implies the change of position of the soles of the feet from the front to the side, be it right or left, or even at times to the back.

F. PATCHES

CLASSIFICATION:

1. PATCHES WITH LOCKS ,
2. SIMPLES,
3. WITH JOINT LOCKS ,
4. WITH THROWS TO THE FLOOR ,
5. WITH FALLS TO THE FLOOR.

The patch technique consists in sticking to your opponent once he is prepared to attack. Just like the bull fighter who sticks to the bull when it is trying to gore him. Example: You first block the foot or the hand that was prepared to strike and then you stick to his body.

From here adequate techniques for each situation are carried out, such as:-
- Feet cuts,
- Dislocations,
- Elbow techniques,
- Knee blows,
- Shoulder blows,
- Head blows, etc.
Leave the combat position with a rapid movement towards the opponent, stop him trying to strike or kick by sticking ourselves to his body.

With this technique we have decreased his potential action by 90%. The surprise factor is a great ally.

41

G. LEG CUTS

DEFINITION

All the leg techniques which are not blows are called leg cuts.

The origin of this technique is in JUDO and other arts. The principal is to grab the opponent or his hands, feet or clothes with one or both hands and direct him, with the purpose of making him lose his balance; while on the other hand, our leg opposes said movement blocking it.
You throw in the same direction as the foot blocks getting ahead of the opponent's foot. The cut may be applied to one foot or to both. Both movements can be done as one, or with certain dead time between them, until the opponent has become unbalanced. The unbalancing of the opponent is always sought so that he may lose weight on the foot in which we are attempting the cut technique.
In any case the key is to unbalance the opponent before we may carry out the foot cut. Very often, pulling or pushing the opponent is enough for him to fall, without it being necessary to apply the second action of the foot cut technique.

H. PRESSURE TECHNIQUES

Pressure techniques are defined as the action of the arms or legs on the lower and upper part of the opponent's leg or arm.

The pressure movement is applied as a single movement and is used especially against attacks which have been initiated with the opponent's hand.

The exception to the rule is the block with our leg on the knee of the opponent.

Once learnt it is a very simple and efficient technique, usually done without position changes.

We are almost talking about a technique of dislocation by blocking and pressure of the joints.

The practise of this marvellous and powerful technique is applied with almost no force.

I. BUTTINGS

WOULD LIKE TO BE TORRO ?

The butting techniques are pushing techniques, performed with the shoulder or the back curved, thus the starting point is from the side or frontal position.
On some occasions it is used as a block with a 180º rotation. It is applied in defence with a block or dodge, in counter-attack following a block or a blow. It may be applied hitting full on the opponent's chest, hitting the middle or lower part of the body or the feet.
On many occasions it is applied very successfully when the aggressor is trying to get nearer with a blow or a kick.
It is the movement that the bull does when attacking.
It is done changing the direction of the attack which will not be from down upwards but face forwards.

The ways of carrying it out may be applied at different levels with movement forwards, backwards or simply in a defence position. To apply this technique at a level lower than the opponent's body, for example, legs, the feet are bent adopting a low position at the same time that we expose the shoulder or the back as point of impact.

J. THROWS

The throw technique is the technique of holding and projecting. They are techniques used in various martial arts.
It is a perfect counter-attack technique used with the rolling technique.
It is applied against blows and kicks.
Composing movements in the throw technique.

1. After the opponent has begun his attack, for example with the hand going past our head, we also move forward, getting hold with both hands the hand that is attacking us.
2. At the same time we situate ourselves with our back to the adversary's abdomen.
3. As you pull the opponent's hand forwards, you raise his body with the hip directing it towards a frontal projection.
4. This may be with or without leg cuts, either frontal or side or to the back.
5. Except the first movement, the rest are performed as one, towards the desired direction.

Throwing techniques have many ways of being performed. For example, with foot hooks, that is, hooking our foot with one of the opponent's feet. There are also throws without the use of the hip, like the one produced by the action of a twist, a simple or double strangling, using the clothes of the other one or our arms.

K. ROLLS

DO YOU WANT TO ROLL YOUR SELF UP ?

Here are some suggestions.

Rolling is the technique of stopping blows or kicks without changing their direction and counter attacking in the opposite direction, or applying a technique following the direction of the attacker's blow, always making the most of the unbalancing created by this or the less stable areas.

The photograph shows the first rolling movement followed by the movement of the right foot to the back until we are almost stuck to the opponent.
Once in this position an elbow blow to the back, to the throat, would fit in perfectly.

L. DODGING

Let's dance!

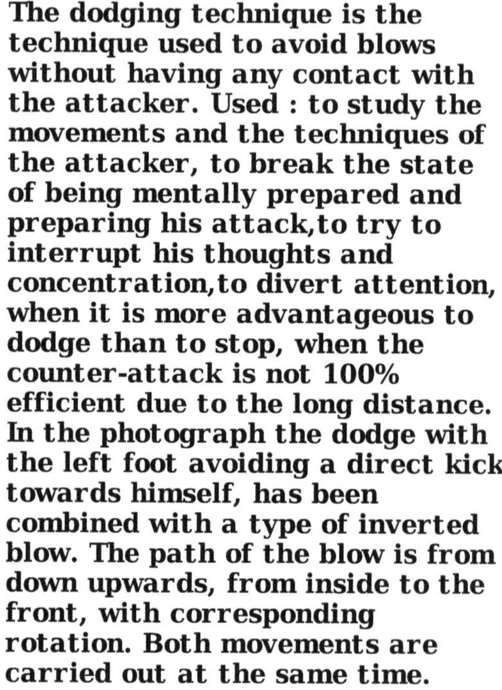

The dodging technique is the technique used to avoid blows without having any contact with the attacker. Used : to study the movements and the techniques of the attacker, to break the state of being mentally prepared and preparing his attack,to try to interrupt his thoughts and concentration,to divert attention, when it is more advantageous to dodge than to stop, when the counter-attack is not 100% efficient due to the long distance. In the photograph the dodge with the left foot avoiding a direct kick towards himself, has been combined with a type of inverted blow. The path of the blow is from down upwards, from inside to the front, with corresponding rotation. Both movements are carried out at the same time.

Another type of dodge used as a defence against a kick aimed at the right foot.
It is a very positive position because from here you can attack in various directions and with an impressive number of blows that can be applied in many areas.
By only extending the right foot and hitting the foot that was attacking, we have managed to defend ourselves with little movement and small use of energy.

This position is often used as a dodge, avoiding a kick towards the head with the hands ready for a counter-attack or second defence.

This position also serves as a dodge against a kick and furthermore the foot is prepared to apply a turning kick towards the opponent's head. With the position of the left foot raised until the knee is situated at the height of the waist, high kicks may be performed.
The position of the hands helps the balance and their movements make the balancing stable and safe.

As the left foot unfolds and kicks, the left arm pulls on an imaginary rope a little towards the back which makes the foot rise and kicks the foot which is in action. The two movements are directly related.

Dodge technique applied together with foot cut against a kick directed at the head. To do this type of combination you must have intuition, precaution and apply the technique once a few moments have passed from the start of the opponent's attack. The foot cut is done with the leg situated in a front position coming from the back, tracing a semi circle. The body rests on the arms leaving the opponent's kick to fall into space, while the opponent's foot no longer has contact with the floor.

M. ATTACK

Attack is recommended:-
When the opponent is between actions, that is, he is mentally preparing his attack, when he shows fatigue, when he is very near, to avoid being in his reach, when there is no other option (the opponent is very close).
When you have more than one adversary, in this situation always attacking first, beginning with the leader or biggest person.
Attacks must be decisive and sure.
In an attack the most suitable technique may be used depending on the situation of combat.
There are no rules or regulations.
Sometimes attack is the best defence, but of course it depends on each particular situation. In 80% of the cases it is preferable to let the opponent attack.
Try to use as little energy as possible and use the maximum energy of your opponent instead.
In the circumstance of a confrontation where you have an opponent experienced in martial arts it is advisable that the attack be composed of various combinations carried out as quickly as possible but with total control.

N. BULTER TECHNIQUES

Would you like to be a dog?

Bulter techniques are aimed at disabling the limb used by the opponent in his attacks. For example, to a hand attack you can apply:
1. a block followed by,
2. the application of pressure techniques,
3. next a knee blow on the elbow, the hand being in an extended position for the application of the pressure technique.
It is understood that the combinations may be continued adding to them those numbered above. All these techniques, applied with the minimum space between them and without letting go of the attacking element, compose the Bulter technique. It is exactly what a bull terrier does when it bites and does not let go. In other words, if with one hand you grab the attacking element, be it a hand or leg.

The other hand applies blow, dislocation, and twisting techniques to it. You get hold of the attacking element with the other hand and continue applying the same blow techniques with the hand that so far was grabbing the attacking element. The action, the technique in itself, may be applied both on the attacking element as on the parts of the body of the opponent.

O. OPPRESSIVE TECHNIQUES

Oppressive techniques are techniques of approaching the opponent quickly and applying strong pushes, blows with the shoulder and the head.
The application area most used is the abdomen.
The technique is applied at the moment in which the opponent is about to or has already begun his attack without giving him time to apply his techniques. The technique is composed of two actions:-
1. The quick approach and,
2. The application of the chosen technique, in movement.

The effect of this technique is to finish with the opponent in record time. Before performing an oppressive technique you must pay attention to the following factors:-

- **cover your plans,**
- **study the state of your opponent in the moment of application,**
- **look in your opponent's eyes,**
- **be oppressive.**

6. Style of performance

Do you want to have style?

The style of performance is one of the most important chapters. I will begin by saying that it is not all just aiming and hitting. Let's take an example:- We have established the target, we have aimed and applied the blow. What happens at the moment of impact? It causes pain and more importantly the part which has been hit moves back. Well then, how much will it move back, will it be to the right or to the left? It depends a lot on the strength applied. I ask you the following: What will happen if we imagine that the target is not really where it is, but some 30 cm further back, more to the right or to the left, and we apply the blow with the intention of reaching the imaginary target?
The consequences of this type of action will be:-
1. the impact will take place much sooner than normal,
2 the speed and the force will rise spectacularly.
3. The performer will try to apply the blow as soon as possible to gain time in performance, thinking that the target is really 30cm further back.
These are just a few of the consequences without going into too much detail. I will ask you a question without giving you the reply. What will happen when you learn to apply blow techniques in this way, knowing what has been explained previously?
In TAUDANC as you are seeing, the mentality is different, the techniques and other components of the style have their own and unique way of performing, a different way of thinking and a modern vision backed up by more than 24 years of practise and study. It is logical that with time, as it has been demonstrated, all styles of martial arts have suffered substantial changes or of little importance. Those which have suffered fundamental changes have been transformed into modern styles without maintaining the original name of the style. Other more conservative styles although having suffered changes, have preferred to keep the original name of the style or add to it one or two more words to the original name of the style.

There are styles that survive time and others which are born having as their base the ancient techniques, but which have suffered substantial changes in regards to the student's behaviour, the teacher's attitude, implementing, decreasing or wiping out old rules and habits as much as from the teacher as from the pupil.

In my opinion I don't believe that one style is better than another but more that between the individuals that are fighting one is better than another. And here we are talking about a complete baggage of aptitudes that each one possesses.

7. Diagrams

Diagrams are ways of showing fighting against one or more imaginary opponents. The idea is to practise and mix the learnt techniques in different ways of performance. It is advisable to practise the diagrams step by step:-
1. Diagrams using hand techniques (blocks, blows, rolls, dodge, butts etc).
2. Diagrams with below the waist techniques, that is, all the techniques that are applied a lower level, be it blocks, foot cuts or other techniques.
3. The practising of the techniques using the dodge as the dominant one.
4. The practising of the techniques with 15 to 45º rotations.
5. The type of diagram having only one opponent. In all the techniques breathing from the abdomen are used, the expelling of air through the mouth at the moment of the blow is controlled by the chest and the throat. Breathing is associated to each blow or kick, the distribution of the power increasing or decreasing according to the strength used depending on the applied technique. This explains that for each blow the breathing will be different as will the power or the volume of breathed in air, in comparison with a kick, a butt or a throw which will make you expel the maximum amount of air, thus making the performance of the technique under discussion more powerful. Also diagrams may be practised in two groups.
Example: -group of block and blow combination,
-group of foot block and counter-attack combination.
-group of dodge and butt,
-group of block and throwing,
-group of block and foot cut,
-group combined only with attacks. The diagrams should not be limited by certain combinations and types of performance, but they must take into account the following factors: breathing, focus, permanent control of the imaginary opponent, balance and complicity. As advice, we wish to say that in the moment of the performing of a block, the hands, feet and all the body must be prepared for the next movement, which may be a counter-attack, another block or the application of any other learnt technique. It is recommended that the performance of the diagrams have a defined space of 5x5 square metres, minimum space allocated for the imaginary fight. The combinations of a diagram are of free choice and are composed by a minimum of 10 movements for a fight with multiple adversaries, reducing to only one combination or one movement that finishes with just one opponent. It is very important not to get overwhelmed and to finish the performance of the diagram. The group: - distribution of breathing, distribution of weight by feet, the situation of balance, protection at all times, preparation of the next movement, the speed and total control of the opponent are very important factors for a correct performance of the TAUDANC style. NOTE:It is recommended that you begin with diagrams composed only of butts, dodges, and direct techniques separately.

8. Training

SUMMARY

Training is composed of:

1. WARMING UP,
- Of the wrists, elbows, knees, waist, neck, sole of foot, shoulder, back.

2. BREATHING,

3. STRETCHING,

4. CONTRACTION AND MUSCLE RELAXATION in this order:_
- Arms and abdomen,
- Arms, pectorals and abdomen,
- Neck ,
- Legs.
Time of contraction, from 5 to 15 seconds followed by 3 to 5 seconds of relaxation.

5. ISOMETRIC EXERCISES,

6. MEDITATION AND RELAXATION 3 minutes sitting down.

7. GENTLE CARRYING OUT OF THE TECHNIQUES with or without partner.

8. IMAGINARY FIGHT GENTLE-SHORT or with partner.

9. FINALISE the training by running for 2 minutes and then relax, lying down on your back in the shape of a cross trying to imagine heaven.

NOTES:

Breathing :

- deep breathing in/breathing out through the nose 5 times, then we repeat covering one nostril and then the other by expelling the air continuously with 80% strength.
Learn to control your breathing. Finalize with one deep breath in and out.
Meditation and relaxation.

Leave your mind free, it deserves 3 minutes rest, don't think about anything, eyes closed, and comfortable position.

After the first 30 seconds, try to imagine that you are holding your arms up to a height of 3 metres. You have to feel that it is hard to keep them up there. With this first exercise you will have work to do for months, until you feel the pain in your arms from the effort used.

Wrist and finger stretching.

The purpose is to prepare the necessary elasticity in the practise of various techniques avoiding accidents and increasing the beauty of the performance. The movement begins with the feet lightly apart, with the hands in front, raised, the palms joined, with the fingers linked together. At this point we will begin to practise the rotation of the hands towards the body and then pushing them towards the front. You will notice the pressure in the fingers and the wrist .It must be a light movement, not forced, going back and forwards.
The elbows move from semi bent position to semi straight position. This is the back and forwards movement.

Put pressure on the wrists.

This serves not only for warming up the wrists but also the muscles of the forearm.
By putting pressure on a palm a pressure force is received, partly by the forearm and the elbow. It is a light exercise that can be practised letting the hands find the ideal point and the exact distance to carry it out.

WooooW ,

Stretching of arms, elbows, wrists with action on the left arm.
The exercise begins with the hands raised to the front, the palms facing outwards, the thumb facing down. The hands join together followed by the intertwining of the fingers. From this position with the fingers intertwined in straight position towards the front, do an inward turn (to the chest) followed by a twisting movement between the arms and fingers towards the front as far as possible. With practise the correct position of stretching is achieved which is the whole extension of the elbows.

To stretch the left elbow,

At the beginning of the exercise the left hand is situated on top of the right hand.
The action is gentle and natural without forcing and without trying to arrive at the maximum extension of the elbows before one week; we consider it a daily practise.
Time must be given for the muscles and ligaments to get flexible.

Practise of flexibility of the wrists inwards.

It is recommended to pay special attention to this practise of flexibility due to:-

- High number of accidents,
- Key point in the carrying out of techniques of aikido, haphido, ju-jitsu on the part of the possible opponent.

Warming up of the waist and back practising the "foot cuts".

Strength of twist 35-45%
As we have already seen, in the performance of this technique it only remains to say that it is not a combat situation, because the focus is centred on the twist of the spine in a gentle and gradual way.

Warming up of the waist and back practising the "foot cuts" to the right.

Strength of twist 35-45% . Focus centred on the twist of the spine in a gentle and gradual way.

Stretching of back and feet. The exercise begins in a straight position with a distance of extension between the legs of 1-1.20 metres, followed by the bending of the body forwards with the hands extended and trying to touch the floor with the palms or with the fists. The practise of this exercise has an effect of back stretching, the ligaments of the legs involved and the strengthening of the back muscles. On arriving in this position, a to and fro movement is made with the hip intervening in the pressure that carries out the movement of the hands towards the floor. Another characteristic that it has is the rocking in short movements towards the floor and at the same time towards the back.

Warming up of the sides of the neck at a 45º angle

The warming up of the neck is carried out in a standing position with the hands resting on the waist doing the following steps:-

The head leans lightly towards the left and the right.
- Putting the head straight, at the start, we look to the right at a 15 to 30º angle followed by a light movement to the back.
The same is done looking to the left.
As a final part we have the very light turn of the head doing complete turns to the right and to the left.

Warming up of the knees inwards and outwards with complete rotation.
From the combat position towards the left return to the front position with a distance of 60-80 cm between the feet, in such a way that when flexing the legs more, the knees have an almost perfect vertical projection with the floor. From this position place the palms on the knees and apply a simultaneous movement of pushing inwards and then towards the back. The exercise must be practised in such a way that the hands act as a guide applying very little force on the knees. Once you have learnt it and are accustomed to the semi turn movement, you must let the knees move easily.

NOTE:
Movement is always inwards and to the back. Once the action is learnt it may be finished with the complete extension of the knees to the back.

Practising opening.
With the practise of opening we are working towards obtaining more flexibility each time up to a reasonable limit that should be maintained all the time. The right hand pushes the hip forwards gently, the left hand resting on the left knee, helping to keep the balance in the short flexing movement.
The soles are firmly place on the ground facing forwards but at an angle of 30-40º to the right. The back is straight, looking forwards. The idea is that with the pressure of the left hand at the same time that the right foot moves carefully back, the effort of the ligaments of the inside legs can be felt. The same exercise is practised changing the position of the feet.

90º stretching with foot underneath,
The correct position is standing with the left sole of the foot forwards, the sole of the right foot to the right, between a distance of 1-1.20 m. without putting too much strain on any muscle or ligament. From this position lower yourself bending totally the right foot, resting it on the sole or the toes. The sole of the left foot will not touch the floor and will rest on the heel, reaching a 100% stretching of the foot. A short movement is carried out with the hip downwards trying to get the muscles used to stretching. Back straight, the right arm helping to maintain the necessary balance in the short downwards movement. The exercise continues with the stretching of the other foot.

Strengthen the muscles and make them resistant.
Five minutes without moving. The spine straight, the back pushed forwards. The distance between the legs is double the width of the shoulders, the legs bent forwards in such a way that they go over what could be considered a perpendicular path to the ground between the knee–toe combination.
A light hip movement (some 10 cms) is also practised towards the floor followed by the return to the initial position. This exercise apart from strengthening the muscles is working other groups of muscles: the abdomen, good movement of the hip, and it gets the spine used to maintaining a correct position. The distance between the soles of the feet may be increased or decreased by 10-15cm. The shoulders are held back but in a natural and light way.

Stretching of the knee.

In standing position: the left foot is bent resting on the top part of the right knee, holding the sole with the right hand, pulling up lightly.
In the meantime, the left hand is pushing lightly downwards and to the right.
The stretch may be practised, at first, resting on a wall until you are able to practise it with the only support being the right foot and the left foot respectively.
The stretching is carried out, once in position, with the foot held, in one push pull movement, in a series of 4-5 movement.

Leg stretching at 90º and of the back with twist to the left

In a sitting position with the legs extended forming an90º angle, bend the right foot towards the body until touching the left foot with the sole. On arriving in this position, hold the toes of the left foot with the left hand while the right hand presses lightly on the right knee obtaining the at the same time the total extension of the left foot and the stretching of the back together with the twist to the left.
From this point, the right hand together with the shoulder carries out a twist to the left and downwards that at first will be limited. The head and the left hand carry out a second movement forwards.
The right hand is used as a support and balance.

Warm up of foot with complete rotations in both directions.

In sitting position, the right foot is situated on the left foot holding it with the left hand, in such a way that the foot is relaxed so that the right hand may carry out complete rotations forwards and back.
The right elbow uses the force transmitted by the right shoulder, in this way maintaining the part of the foot parallel to the floor. This way other groups of muscles can be worked.
Optional: To increase the difficulty of the exercise you can try to get closer by bending the back in an attempt to touch the foot which is rotating, with the forehead.

Total stretching of the legs.
From the position previously mentioned, raising the right foot and pulling it back until the position in the photograph is arrived at. Try to maintain an angle of 90º angle which is considered to be the correct position of the back with the floor, at the same time that the right hand keeps the right foot towards the back still and the left hand moves lightly and maintains the straight position of the left foot, achieving the necessary balance to keep the position. It is recommended that it should be practised for about 5 minutes.
As a continuation to this exercise we try to bend the back in the direction and the length of the left foot or towards the front by using a gentle and slow back and forwards movement. Repetitions of 5 times back and forwards are recommended of muscles can be worked.

Stretching of:

- Opening angle,
- Back,
- Neck,
- Shoulders,
- Feet,
- Spine.

The exercise has the stretching of the hands upwards action while the elbows press downwards on the legs together with the bending of the spine downwards until the head touches the feet, keeping them together with the hands.
It is a group of movements that are carried out as if one to and fro.
Stretching must be practised without straining.
Get weekly results.

Warming up of the hip

From the basic position with the palms situated on the hips, the right hand pushes the hip back making the right foot do a complete extension.
The body leans to the right at a 45º angle at the same time that the left foot bends lightly.
Repetitions are practised 7-8 times, and then you change foot.
The body should lean forwards in the direction of the foot with which it is practising the extension, as much as necessary, but without forcing.
We are only warming up the parts of body.

As an additional option, from this position the right foot will go from resting on all of the sole to only resting on the toes with the heel raised.
From this moment, the hip is swivelled around the imaginary perpendicular line to the floor.
The movement may have a wide radius or a natural one (whatever the body allows).

Stretching of the shoulder with twist of the hip.

Performance: - from this base position the hands are raised with the thumbs almost joined, the elbows semi extended above the head as high as the arms will allow, and the palms facing forwards.
The following movement consists in a twist of the spine to the left with the palms facing up without changing the initial position of the soles.

The movement should be done to the two sides with a pause between them and in repetitions of 5 times.
With this exercise the abdomen will also be strengthened.

Stretching of shoulders and contraction of the spine.

From the base position with the hands extended to the front the fingers are intertwined, following from a turning movement to the outside-forwards. From here, you pass to the raising of the hands until they reach head level pushing lightly upwards. Follow the movement with your eyes from the beginning to the end. The back suffers a light contraction because of the pressure of the hands going up and back. This may be done in slow or very slow repetitions of 5-6 complete times. It can be combined with a back twist, trying to reach as close to the floor as possible with the palms, extending the knees to the maximum.

Stretching of the abdomen and pectorals. Returning to the initial position we place ourselves at a distance of 30 cm between the soles. Arms extended, with the palms facing forward, you begin to bend the spine back making a semicircle between the head and the heels of the feet. The palms act as a counter balance as if they had weights. From this point, with the necessary balance the heels of the feet are lifted and the body rests on the toes. The second part of this exercise consists in the raising of the heels and return to the floor. The points which are worked are the abdomen, pectorals, the feet and the back of the neck; you must not go over the semi circle traced by the spine and the feet. It is one of the positions of glory of the bull fighter interpreted TAUDANC Style.

ISOMETRIC EXERCISES

They are exercises that have the effect of putting into action certain groups of muscles. All these exercises are done positioned under an open door frame.

The object on which the force is applied firstly is the door frame so that later it can be done with the imaginary frame.
The exercise consists of applying pressure on objects, using for this, parts of the body beginning with the hands, legs and back. The simplest exercises consist of: - pushing out, - pushing up, - pulling in.
Various combinations can be carried out as we will see next.
The strength used is of 10-15% and the duration of each exercise does not exceed 10 seconds.

Pushing up to the sky.

Situating ourselves in basic position under a door frame try to push the top part of the frame up. Look at the action of the push.

Getting out of the crowd

The exercise consists in pushing with the left hand up and out and the right hand down and back. The feet are situated in line, with the soles facing to the left. The position of the head, in times of 5 seconds moves to the right, to the left and to the front. Remember that what the hands are pushing are the door frames so give it the necessary force.

Making space for yourself.

The same movement, another position, another group of muscles to work.

Closing doors.

With this exercise we aim to strengthen the fingers, the wrist, shoulders, pectorals and cervical.

With the fingers hold the outside of the sides of the door frame and pull inwards. The position of the body will be 20 cm in front of the door frame.

Blocking the doors

Situated under the door frame with the palms in a fist we rest the forearms on the side frames and we begin to push outwards taking into account the previously specified force.

Open doors

This exercise aims at working other groups of muscles actioned by the pressure from the palms towards the outside.
The body is situated some 20 cm from the frame.

To finalize the exercise we apply a stretching to the front of legs and spine.
The exercise is practised with the help of a chair or other object that can be used as a rest for the foot.

Stretching of the foot by flexing.

It can be practised with the sole of the foot facing the front, with the toes facing up or with the foot in position of side blow.

9. Weapons

The majority of martial arts use weapons as an addition respecting ancient customs.

The TAUDANC weapons are: - the ball and the nunchakus.
The ball is a simple weapon, but efficient. It may be a golf ball with a hole made in it, where a fine and elasticised wire is introduced and tied/stuck. It is a wire of some 25 cms long and is tied to one of the fingers.
The practise is very simple and is learnt quickly. With this weapon back and forward blows are applied on the sensitive points such as: face, neck, hands, legs and abdomen. It is very useful in combination with dodging, blocking and attack techniques.
The nunchakus: weapon composed of two sticks, joined by a chain or a short rope.

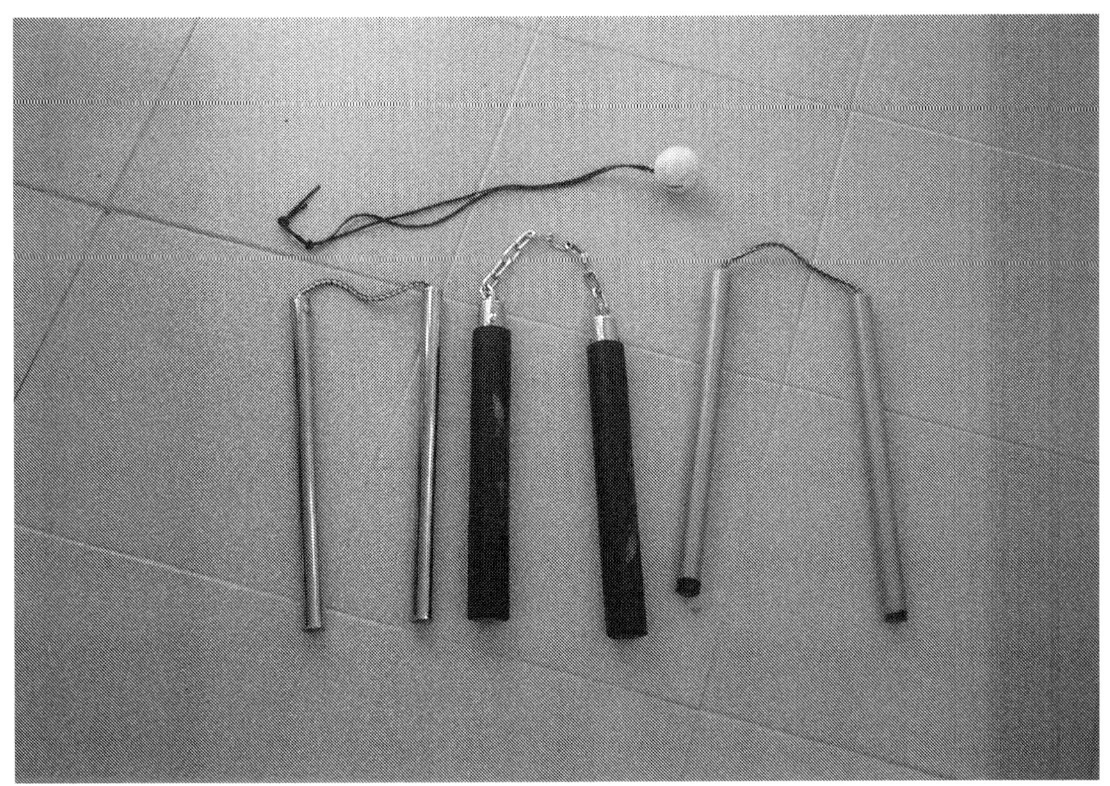

10. Style & Health

This chapter refers to the way of carrying out the techniques you have learnt in a very slow way. They may be combinations freely chosen that will be practised with natural breathing accentuating the exhaling at the moment of the execution of the blow, block, kicks (waist down).

It is preferable to memorize a series of different combinations from the techniques that are practised in the diagrams.
Health comes from the practise of these exercises of controlled breathing, using various types of breathing in, depending on the chosen techniques, characterised by the way of working the muscles and the other parts of the body in a very slow way. It is a technique very different to the rest.
It is very important that in each movement breathing or inhaling of different intensity is applied.
Example:
In the performing of a block and counter-attack with displacement we will have three types of breathing:
In the moment of blocking, the expelled air to strengthen it will be 40% of intensity with the vocalisation of the letters "a" and "s".

The expelled air, when performing a counter-attack (a hand blow towards the chest), will be between 30-60% intensity, vocalising the letters "aia". Next turn towards the right in an imaginary situation opposite three opponents. At the moment of the withdrawal and turn an expelling of air of 10% intensity is done vocalising "a", being now prepared for the next movements.

For an easy execution, we may begin with the idea of practising a diagram very slowly of free choice and composition, in which perfection is sought and control of the movements associated to one or various types of breathing in and breathing out.

It must be mentioned that the correct execution will take its time, taking into account that it is a technique totally different to the rest and because it improves your health.
This achievement is explained by the different way of treating the muscles and ligaments and most importantly the applied breathing, which is totally controlled and measured.
A very important factor is the observation of the imaginary situation you

have created, and the free study and action of combat.
By this I mean that for the beginner it is much easier to get used to practising TAUDANC in its entirety, controlling the situation of imaginary combat and self control.

It is like watching a film in slow motion with the possibility of intervening and changing things as many times as we wish, because we are the script writers.

The progress and skill of this practise depends on the intellectual capacity of each student.
It is really a dance in slow motion with much use of the lungs, combination of rotations, turns and the most important, the pass from defence to attack or from dodging to butting very slowly, smoothly without interruptions between the techniques chosen to be carried out.
It is advisable to carry out a chain of mixed techniques.

Do I need a Chinese outfit?

Well ,sheep pyjamas work well for me!

11. Tools for Training

1. Straw sack or cushion.

2. Wide belt with sand,

3. Chair,

4. Small rug

5. Ball,

6. Nunchaku,

7. Light clothing,

The straw sack may be fastened to a wall.
The belts with sand are worn tied to the wrists and ankles during the practise of the techniques.
The tools for training are objects that are used:-

- To increase speed

- To improve performance of the techniques.

- To get the body accustomed to the strength of this style.

- To increase performance,

- To help stretch,

- To practise getting accustomed to the training method and its applications.

The end result of using the tools is to strengthen the body, once the training has finished, you should feel light and nimble.

12. Quick learning Course

The quick learning course is composed of a series of combinations of easy techniques because of their order of execution, selected with the aim of helping the student. The strength used is of 25-30%, speed 50%. Attention to the control of the breathing.

Example nº 1:

1. Frontal blow
2. Inverted blow
3. Simple block
4. Blow with the knuckles
5. Dodge
6. Dodge and knuckle blow
7. "Goose neck" block"

Example nº 2:

1. Basic position

2. Simple block to the right with the side of the hand.
3. Hammer blow to the right.
4. Hard block and frontal blow.

5. Side kick
6. Basic position

Example nº 3:

1. Basic position
2. Kick block with the leg
3. Side kick
4. Combat position
5. Side kick to the femur.(stopping blow)
6. Block and straight blow
7. Basic position

Example nº 4:

1. **Basic position**
2. **Kick to the back**
3. **Butting with shoulder**
4. **Kick block**
5. **Elbow block**
6. **Elbow blow**
7. **Frontal kick**
8. **Basic position**

13. Comments

There are many cases which we can comment on but we are just going to add some explanations to the chapters of this first book.

The chapter STYLE AND HEALTH shows how all the techniques can be practised with slow movements, Tai-Chi style, of which everybody has heard.

Diagrams may be carried out, your own combinations or selections of series of only blocks, only kicks, foot cuts etc. This slow way of practising the techniques apart from improving health, gets you used to doing things without a hurry, and most importantly makes you create combinations and carry them out slowly without interruption as you go along.

It is not important if beforehand you have written down some techniques, to practise, because always, once they have been done, you will be tempted to continue with something else.

The idea in itself of Tai-Chi is that of a snake that bites its tail, which means that the action is circular, that you say when it ends.

I don't recommend you memorizing a certain exercise "x" to repeat every day, on the contrary once you have learnt the technique let your imagination free and you will be surprised by the attractive combinations that you are capable of composing.
Practising TAUDANC, at a given time, it must be understood that it is not about who is better or which the worse style is.

This is about yourself, of how you feel. What has brought you to TAUDANC? Do you feel comfortable practising it? Has it produced a positive change in your life? Has your health improved?

These are some real questions that one should ask themselves after a few weeks of training.
Many comments can be made about THE TECHNIQUES AND THE PHILOSOPHY OF TAUDANC, but the important thing is to start.

Do you remember about learning to learn?

14. Bonus

In the next Book :

Master Techniques

GLOSSARY

B BUTTS – Bull techniques of pushing.

D DIRECT TECHQNIQUES- two techniques performed as one

D DODGES – techniques of avoidance

H HOOK KICK- transformations of the foot in a drag hook.

I ISOMETRIC EXERCISES- form of contracting and relaxing muscles.

L LEG CUTS- techniques designed to throw to the floor by unbalancing.

P PATCHES- technique of sticking to opponent.

P PRESSURE TECHNIQUES- specific joynt locks and breaking techniques.

Q QUICK LEARNING COURSE- easy combinations for beginners.

R ROTATORY KICKS- kick carried out with the rotation of the body.

S SELF DEFENCE AND HEALTH- integral part of TAUDANC STYLE.

S SPANISH MARTIAL ARTS (TAUDANC)

S STYLE OF PERFORMANCE- idea originating from TAUDANC

T TAUDANC- new style of martial arts.

T THROWING- techniques of grabbing and throwing.

T TRAINING- specific to the style.

W WARNING- addressed to the people that may suffer damage without consulting a doctor before beginning practise.

W WEAPONS- tools used with the purpose of training arms, wrists and other parts of the body.

As it is a Spanish style of self defence ,all the words being in English mean exactly what they say.

INDEX

Martial Map.

Japan – more than 20 types of Martial Arts.
Korea- more than 4 types
China- more than 2000 styles and branches
Brazil- Capoeira, Brazilian ju-jitsu

Southern Asia,

India- Kalaripayattu,
Philippines- Eskrima, Kali Eskrima,
Thailand – Muay- Thai (Thai Boxing),
Indonesia and Malaysia - Pentjak silat
South America
Capoeira, Brazilian ju-jitsu.

Europe

France-Savate
Greece- Pankration, Greek roman fighting.
Ireland- Bataireacht,
Spain- TAUDANC with others which have been borrowed.

Almost each country has its own martial arts, but the majority of the countries are practising martial arts borrowed from other cultures.
The difference being that those who have their own martial arts as a national sport or a treasure from their ancestors are filled with pride.

www.ingramcontent.com/pod-product-compliance
Ingram Content Group UK Ltd.
Pitfield, Milton Keynes, MK11 3LW, UK
UKHW051128260726
13967UKWH00010B/2933